BIBLE FAMILIES

Joseph and His Brothers

Linda and Alan Parry

AUGSBURG
MINNEAPOLIS, USA

HUNT & THORPE
ALTON, UNITED KINGDOM

'Joseph is the greatest,' said his father Jacob.
And Joseph strolled around in a brilliant coat
his father had given him.
But Joseph's ten half brothers couldn't
stand him.

'You're all going to bow down to me,' Joseph said. 'I've dreamed about it.'

'That's what you think!' his brothers sneered.

One day the brothers were miles away from home with their sheep when they saw Joseph coming toward them. Alone.
'Here's the dreamer!' they said. 'Come on. Kill him.'

They seized Joseph and threw him in a pit.
Then they saw some traders on their way
to Egypt.

'Even better,' they said. 'Sell him.'

Good riddance. That's the last of Joseph.
They smeared his coat with goat's blood.

'Look what we found,' they said to Jacob.
Jacob thought Joseph had died, and cried.

In Egypt God was with Joseph.
Pharoah the king had a strange dream. Only
Joseph knew its meaning.

'There will be seven years of good harvests
followed by famine,' he said.

'The country needs a man of God like you,'
said Pharoah. 'You can be in charge of
emergency operations.'

During the years of plenty Joseph stored up all the spare grain.

The famine came.
'There's food in Egypt,' Jacob said. 'Go and
buy some.'

Off went the ten brothers. They left Joseph's younger brother, Benjamin, safe with Jacob.

The brothers bowed low before Joseph, Governor of all Egypt. They did not know he was their brother.

But Joseph recognized
them and remembered his dream.
'Who are you? Where are you from? You've
got to be spies,' he yelled.

Joseph had to find out if his brothers were as rotten as ever. So he took one brother, Simeon, for a hostage.

'Come back with Benjamin,' he shouted.

Back home, the brothers were scared to go to Egypt again. But after a while they needed more food, so they went back.

Trembling in their sandals, they bowed down.
'Don't hurt Benjamin,' they cried. 'Our father
loves him.'
Then Joseph knew they had changed.

'Look at me,' he said. 'I'm Joseph. Don't be upset. It was God who sent me to Egypt to save you all from starving. Hurray for God!'

You can read this story in the Bible
in Genesis 37:2−36; 39:1−45:28.

Copyright © 1990 Hunt & Thorpe

First published by **Hunt & Thorpe** in the United Kingdom, 1990
ISBN 1 85608 070 6
and by **Augsburg** in North America, 1990
ISBN 0-8066-2488-4, LCCN 90-80557
The CIP catalogue record for this book is available from the British Library.

Manufactured in Great Britain.